Snow

Honor Head

QED Publishing

First published in the UK in 2006 by
QED Publishing
A Quarto Group company
226 City Road
London EC1V 2TT
www.qed-publishing.co.uk

ISBN 1 84538 359 1

Written by Honor Head
Designed by Melissa Alaverdy
Consultant Terry Jennings
Editor Hannah Ray
Picture Researcher Joanne Forrest Smith
Illustrations Chris Davidson
Diagrams Jonathan Vipond

Publisher Steve Evans
Editorial Director Jean Coppendale
Art Director Zeta Davies

Printed and bound in China

Picture credits

Key: t = top, b = bottom, c = centre, l = left, r = right, FC = front cover

Alamy/ David R Frazier Photolibrary Inc. 5b;
Corbis/ Nathan Benn 9t, /Richard Berenholtz 6,
/John Conrad 14–15, /Tony Demin 17,
/George McCarthy 7, /Don Mason 4–5,
/David Stoecklein 16, /Jim Zuckermann 11;
FLPA/Jurgen & Christine Sohns 14c,
/Roger Wilmshurst 12b;
Getty Images/Shannon Fagan 19, /Gary Holscher 13,
/Tom Morrison FC, 1, /Barbara Peacock 18,
/Kim Westerskov 15t.

Words in **bold** can be found in the glossary on page 22.

Contents

What is Snow?

Snow falls from the clouds.
It snows when it is very cold.

Snow is white and wet and cold. If you go outside when it snows, you need to wear warm winter clothes.

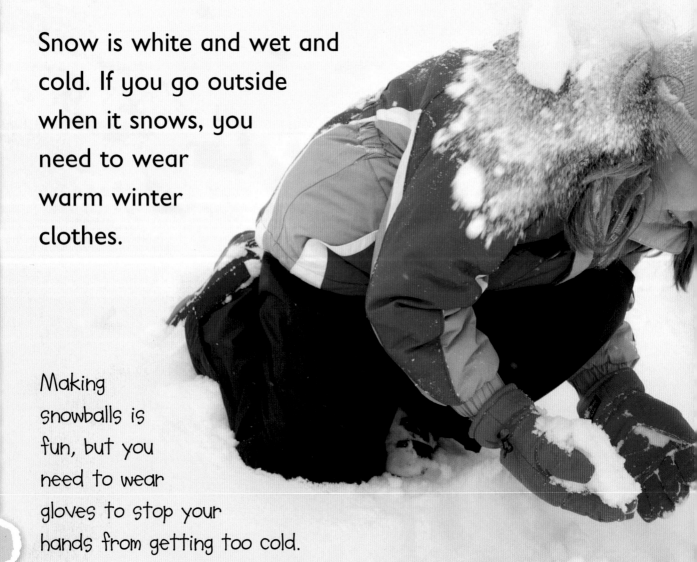

Making snowballs is fun, but you need to wear gloves to stop your hands from getting too cold.

If the snowfall is light, the snow melts when it lands on the ground or when the sun shines. If a lot of snow falls, it settles and makes everything look white.

When it is cold and snowy, you can see your breath in the air.

When Does it Snow?

It usually snows during winter.

This is the time of year when the weather is often cold and windy. It gets darker earlier in the day, and the days are shorter.

In winter, most of the trees have lost their leaves and plants stop flowering. Many birds **migrate** to warmer countries.

During winter, it is dark when you wake up in the morning.

Some animals, such as this dormouse, **hibernate** in the winter when there is not much food.

It is difficult for birds and other animals to find food when it is cold and the ground is frozen.

Where Does Snow Come From?

When it is freezing cold high in the sky, **water droplets** turn into tiny ice crystals. These fall to the Earth as snowflakes.

1. **Water vapour** rises from lakes, ponds, seas and puddles and turns into ice crystals.

2. Ice crystals form clouds.

3. Ice crystals fall back to Earth as snowflakes.

Sometimes, when it is very windy and freezing cold, we have a **blizzard**.

When it is very cold, a lot of snow will fall and cover everything in a white blanket.

Snowflakes

Snow is made up of snowflakes.

All snowflakes have six sides or six points, but each snowflake has a different pattern from the others.

Sometimes in winter, we have sleet. Sleet is a mixture of snow and rain. It can also be made of snow which has started to melt as it falls from the clouds.

During a cold night, everything is covered in a thin white layer that looks like snow. This is **frost**. It sparkles in the morning sunlight.

Every single snowflake
looks different.

Cold as Ice

When the temperature drops and it is very cold, water can freeze and turn into ice.

During winter, the surface of lakes, ponds and puddles is often covered in a layer of ice.

When snow settles it can also turn into ice. This makes it very slippery and you have to be careful when you walk on it.

When lakes and ponds freeze over, water birds cannot get food from the water until the ice melts.

During very cold weather, dripping water freezes before it falls to the ground. This forms icicles, which can be very beautiful.

Cold All Year

In some parts of the world, it is very cold all the time.

These places are called the Arctic and the Antarctic. They are covered in snow and ice for most of the year.

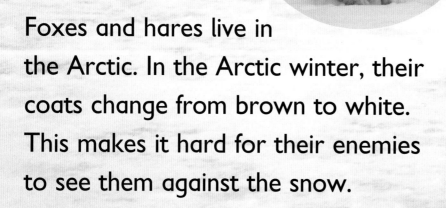

Foxes and hares live in the Arctic. In the Arctic winter, their coats change from brown to white. This makes it hard for their enemies to see them against the snow.

Penguins
live in the
Antarctic.
When there is a
snowstorm, penguins huddle
together in a group to keep warm.

Polar bears
live in the Arctic.
Their thick, furry coats help to keep them warm.

Mountain Snow

Many countries have mountains so high that they are covered in snow all the time, even in summer.

During the winter, many people visit these mountains for skiing holidays. People also enjoy mountain climbing.

People like to snowboard where there is deep snow. This is like surfing in the snow.

Skiing in the mountains is really fun. Children start on an easy ski slope, called a nursery slope.

High up in the mountains, where the snow is very thick, avalanches can happen. This is when snow starts sliding down the mountains in huge lumps. It gets faster and faster. This can be very dangerous if you are caught in its path.

Fun in the Snow

You can have lots of fun in the snow.

If you live near a hill, you can go **tobogganing**. Building a snowman is fun, too.

Always keep warm when you are playing outside in the snow.

Try making your own
snow angel next time it snows.

If the snow is thick, lie down. Move your arms
up and down by your sides, and your legs in
and out. This is called making snow angels.

Have a Snow Party

Use the snowflake template to make invitations for your snow party.

Draw the snowflake onto a thin piece of white card or a small paper plate.

Write the address and time of the party on the other side.

To Hannah

Come to my snow party!

7 Cat Close
Pink Lanes
at 3 o'clock

Wear something white!

Snowball lucky dip

Cover a big box
in white paper.
Buy small presents.
Wrap them in
shiny paper. Put
them in the box
and ask your
friends to dip in
and pick a present.

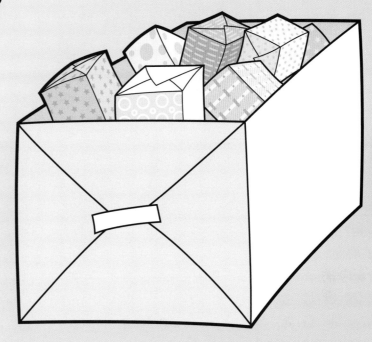

How many snowflakes?

These are not really
snowflakes, but white mini
marshmallows. Put as many
as you can into a jar. Your
friends have to guess how
many there are. The winner
gets a small prize. When you
have played the game, ask
an adult to make some hot
chocolate and sprinkle the
white marshmallows on top.

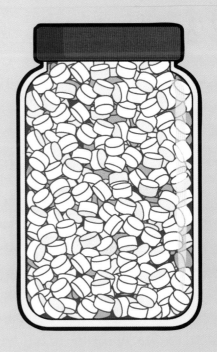

21

Glossary

blizzard   when it snows very heavily and there is a strong, freezing-cold wind.

frost   frost is made up of millions of tiny white ice crystals. It usually settles overnight when the air is colder.

hibernate   some animals sleep, or hibernate, throughout the winter. They wake up in the spring, when the weather is warmer and it is easier to find food.

migrate   when birds or other animals travel to warmer countries.

tobogganing   sliding down snow-covered hills on a sledge, or toboggan.

water droplets   drops of water which are so tiny you can hardly see them.

water vapour   a gas, like steam, which forms when water is warmed.

Index

Parents' and Teachers' Notes

- Look at the cover of the book. Discuss the title and the picture on the cover. Read the back cover. What do the children think the book is about?

- Talk to the children about their memories of snow. When was the last time they saw snow? Was it at home or on holiday? What type of snow was it? Did it settle or did it melt straight away? Did it turn into slush? Explain that slush is snow that has begun to melt.

- Look at the pictures in the book of people playing in the snow. Ask the children about snow games or sports they have played. When did they do these activities? Where? Did they enjoy them? What is their favourite thing to do in the snow?

- Look at the clothes that the children are wearing in the pictures. Name them. Talk about what the children wear in the winter to help keep them warm.

- Look at the photos of animals and talk about how different animals live in cold and snowy places.

- Ask the children to find cards or photos of snow scenes. Pin them up on the wall.

- Make winter decorations with snowflake trails. Ask the children to make a paper snowflake each. String the snowflakes together and hang them up.

- Keep a winter weather diary.

- Look through the book and list all the snowy words, for example, 'white', 'freezing', 'frost', 'cold', etc. What other snow-related words can the children think of? Choose four words and ask the children to write a poem or short story using these words.

- Make a snow scene using papier mâché, cotton wool, plain white paper, white tissue paper, etc. Make a white landscape with some hills and fields. Make white trees. Add some little snowmen.

- Look at the word 'snowman'. How many other words can the children make from this word? For example, 'snow', 'man', 'now', 'won', 'no', 'on', 'saw'.